Nóra Ružičková is a pioneering experimental poet in Slovak literature. She debuted in the late 1990s with her first poetry collection, *Mikronauti* (Micronauts, 1998), which blends her interests in visual arts, feminism and poetry. Her work often explores self-scrutiny as a means of investigating language and the world. Over time, her poetry has increasingly reflected conceptual and post-conceptual influences. Ružičková is also an intermedia artist, translator and teacher. She has published seven poetry collections and co-authored two volumes with artist Marianna Mlynárčiková.

Ivana Hostová is a translator, critic and translation studies scholar affiliated with the Institute of Slovak Literature at the Slovak Academy of Sciences and the Department of Translation Studies at Constantine the Philosopher University in Nitra, Slovakia. Her research integrates various theoretical perspectives, including ecocriticism, gender studies, sociology, political economy, psychoanalysis, critical theory and posthumanism. As a translator into English, she focuses on Slovak poets working in modernist and post-conceptual traditions.

THE SLOVAK LIST

NÓRA RUŽIČKOVÁ

What Now Is Now Is Now

Selected Poems

SELECTED BY
IVANA HOSTOVÁ AND **NÓRA RUŽIČKOVÁ**

TRANSLATED BY
IVANA HOSTOVÁ

COMPARATIVE EDITING BY **MICHAL TALLO**
ADDITIONAL EDITING BY **JOHN MINAHANE**

LONDON NEW YORK CALCUTTA

Slovenské
literárne
centrum

This book was published with the financial support of the
SLOLIA Board, The Slovak Literary Centre.

THE SLOVAK LIST
Series Editor: Julia Sherwood

Seagull Books, 2025

Originally published in Slovak, 1998–2021

© Nóra Ružičková, 2025

First published in English translation by Seagull Books, 2025

English translation © Ivana Hostová, 2025

ISBN 978 1 8030 9 565 3

British Library Cataloguing-in-Publication Data
A catalogue record for this book is available from the British Library

Typeset at Seagull Books, Calcutta, India

CONTENTS

Micronauts   1
- [A red dot]   3

Sedimentation   5
Intonation   6
Marble stitches   7
- [smiling at vegetables]   8
- [The combination]   9
- [Caught a scent]   10
- [From the voyage beyond]   11
- [A single uncovering of the ear]   12

elementary stories   13
- [hangings of skin envelop]   14

Tingle   15
Warp and Weft   17
( ) [At the edge of the field and the meadow]   19
( ) [One side is tirelessness]   23
( ) [The part of the landscape]   24
( ) [So perfectly wrapped up]   25
(Universal Good Feeling)   26
(Albino)   27
( ) [I bite an apple]   28
(Trompe-l'œil)   29
(Breathing Exercise)   30
( ) [there is the density of locks]   31
( ) [As I describe a non-existent drawing]   32
(A Weight)   33

(Performance with Lazarus)	34
( ) [Between me and the object of research]	36
(today, another step)	37
( ) [Including a tiny fault]	38
(This forest this garden)	39

Facelessness — 41

– [All that compacts itself]	43
– [(perhaps) I'll essay myself]	44
– [May I? May I come at rest here?]	45
– [almost / in the tightest closeness]	46
– [fluent is the water]	47
– [Diverting attention I describe myself]	48
– [For only where I lose my firm contours]	49
– [at the beginning I erect a wall]	50
– [skin skinned in skintight]	51
– [what are you mixing?]	52
– [a hit in the invisible]	53
– [squatting at the edge, I lift creatures]	54
– [countless voices have spoken inside me]	55
– [my morning feels as if it was snowing]	56
– [face open in a protective gesture]	57
– [under the touch of the word]	58
– [as I speak I change into]	59
– [now, I do not wish to know]	60
– [there: where I have never been before]	61
– [What is necessarily above the surface]	62
– [face down]	63
– [north, as the destination]	64

- [come to me—stay away] 65
- [I stretch arms into void] 66
- [*we can watch the movie*] 67
- [you say that gestures] 69

Parcelling Out the Air 71

panther 73
a shell 74
shiver 75
livid 76
parcelling out the air 77
tulips 78
bulbs 79
roundness 80
sweet and dear 81
happyend 82
beckett's horses 83
public park 84
coastal research 85
calligraphy 86
dragonflies 87

Coastal Research 89

~ [on the way to the destination] 90
~ [in the hotel room] 91
~ [fatigue duplicates] 92
~ [in the middle of the city] 93
~ [reaching out I wish] 95
~ [the thing in between] 96
~ [surfaces shapes bodies] 97

dreams of rooms	99
~ [yes of course]	100
~ [between me]	101
coastline	102
~ [learning by heart]	103

Works & Intimacy — 105

*** [the carpet wears out]	107
*** [once the stain dries]	109
*** [allergic rash]	110
*** [choose very wisely]	111
*** [banana stains on children's clothes]	112
*** [crystal will be clear and sparkling again]	113
Tianni is truly a natural beauty with a kind, sweet and caring spirit	114
Celeste is the mum, so we're gonna make her glamorous	115
Coralie has vivacious personality and a very big and kind heart	116
A Public Dictionary of Intimacy	117

Contemporaneities — 123

[this is about revival]	1953
[in Želiezovce, Galanta, Trnava, and Hadovce]	1988
[even today, there are regions in Slovakia]	1922
[the avalanche once in motion is hard to stop]	1968
[talking about the engagement of art]	1972
[we are going through difficult times]	1944
[today even politicians understand]	2012
[the economy]	1990

[let's harness the zeal of the young]	1939
[modern technology really demands]	1957
[as university employees]	2020
[the ones who come after you]	1961
[option I]	1969
[the time is ripe for change]	1948
[today we must clean the temple of art of insects]	1925

Micronauts
(1998)

●

A red dot
white circle round it
all wrapped in pink
blurred and soft

a rose in time
exposing countless layers
in the wound

the wound a space of self-projections
the knot (in it) touching self

hands connect
a knot of life lines
the hand of a newborn and of an old man
their images merged (in it)

suddenly you see yourself in the mirror
not looking at yourself
focusing on detail
ignoring the whole

submerge it all in darkness
light an arrow
pointing to the sole space of serenity
among numerous crime scenes

ice and brightness beneath it

something unfolding in a swirl
in this spot of light

a small angel in a radiant womb

all black stockings
hung lap down
above your sleeping child
like guardian animals

above your naked child
hangs an ice egg

on your wonder child
drops drip
tip down
scratching at the air
you both breathe

Sedimentation

A sterile corridor
I sweep a cottonwool ball across the floor
it creaks like an old knee
the white remains
immaculate as conception

Three layers of time:

      The oldest one presents
      a bruise
      proud of the painting
      made in agony

            The middle one, my screen
            steps on my eyelids
            feeling like a guardian

                  Light spots are unbearable
                  and the faces of knees, their eyes lower
                  won't help
                  cheeks whipped by stalks

Intonation

Fragile
perfectly decalcified
absolved of ability
to understand meanings
you arch through me
in deep stitches

crave the bittersweet

so slowly

immensely slowly

divide me

Marble stitches

I was starting to feel
smooth and firm
precisely outlined
meanwhile my hair:

a drawing made by a magnet
temporary mummification
intensity of feelings on a single side
a halo from a vicious circle

The path you take
is a tongue under anaesthetic
the love you make
a tongue hooked:

pull slowly to bifurcate

•

smiling at vegetables
with re-nude sensitivity
I peel it chop it shred it
touch it . . .
the horizon curves
                shaped by hand
so that tenderness doesn't slide
face to heart
or from heart
so that the poem
and lace
undone
evenly long threadlines
are
knots in the wound

●

    The combination
    of flowers and snow
    in women's poetry
red and white
        blood on the dissecting table
        surgically precise chiaroscuro

    What to write on skin
    so that it would be worthwhile
to cut
    insert hooks
    and flay?

    Under snow
    under ground
    under skin
    small carrots
    smooth and shiny baby fingers
    reaching for something deeply dark

●

Caught a scent:
        alien seeds colonize the pot
        new roots tangled with the old ones
        finely
        following a bright model
        they investigate the bed
        the palate with their tongue
        unsettling a simile
        words twist
        like a dead man's pearly buttons
        roots and branches
        over ground as underground
        images growing together with their models

•

From the voyage beyond the reach of the   eye
paid for with the coin of the pupil:

Sunny is seemingly safe

The local scale enlargement
comes from micromythological gleanings

How does one distinguish the movement of the observer
from the movement of the observed
if the whole is a detail of a detail?

●

A single uncovering of the ear
revealed the nudity
of the image burgled by words

In a two-sided illusion of space
funnel-shaped pain

In the recognition of the self as the vanishing point
a contrary illusion of the observer

A single uncovering of the task
concealed two-sided nudity

elementary stories

I'm somebody's option determined by fatigue
I slim down as the universe expands and

> mark the focus of infection lashing out
> disrupt the structure of a fly
> freeze in the moment

I'm a trap for missing the moment

> stone envelops water
> circles concentrically diminish
> characters in the story morph into signs

I crawl out of the hole between words

> mark water lashing out
> disrupt the circle
> freeze in the story

●

hangings of skin envelop
folds to the rhythm of feelings
biuniqueness (a fissure)
I fall into the wound instead of falling asleep

the embryo in the sky
becomes the new moon

shadows of insects under the skin
shivering letters
at the end of the day

drip by drip I petrify
stub out the cigarette on the wall of the pit

the moon grows in me

during the day a melody
for the sake of harmony
in a dream several
overlapping stories

in the body strong spotlights
full weight
falling on my eyelids
tiny insect corpses

Tingle

the snuggling of the ear against the heart
the cupping of the small breasts
with no space for heartbeat

The Last Supper swapped for
a visualization ECG-style

I carry pain to the surface of the body
cut and crystallize

experience and write down simultaneously

touch
and avoid erogenous zones on purpose
in accordance with the aesthetics of my manifesto

smooth face on a hairy chest
eyes in a world of gigantic grasses

Warp and Weft
(2000)

( )

At the edge of the field and the meadow
one mode of plant being permeates another
in various spaces beings
non-communicating islands
and yet on each of them a found statue of co(s)mic squatting

articulate the non-intersection by needle's mouth
                            drip through the eye

hold an apple
under cold running water
until the difference in temperatures disappears
hand—bites—apple—grows

balance reached prematurely   —larger dress   —to the small one
                                —smaller dress —to the large one
it begins and ends with spilling a full glass
a sudden undressing of the face
in one stroke
I connect vessels
(better slowly than too close)
the inner wall of the cup
the upper lip
the inside of the mouth (tongue)
the lower lip
        down
the outer wall of the cup
on the back
        cold half-moon
the haptics of fear
        eyeless flat land

'coldness' enters if the link is not tight enough
                                the word transformed to:
                                'apple section and the surface
in the cup are one'

if the natural environment is the chest   —rip it out
                                         —let it hang
                                         —feel its own weight
enlarge blood vessels (un)identify objects
in the space of the room
curve-machine-release-heart beating on
the tabletop—position the door horizontally
the lock overgrows
forgets the shape
and the door the space in front of it the space behind it
is not perceived
it perceives
the remnants of perfection like phantom pain

children's babble sown
fully enjoy the wait
              un-enhanced
              un-bearable
              un-
                    -grown
darkstill
cotton wool
(in retrospect)
              5 shapelessness
              4 facelessness
              3 two-sided face
              2 two-sided mask
              1 too close

                                                I'll play a trick and you'll
         inhale me
                                                                    outside
                                                                     inside
                                                                    inwood

slowed down in the manner of a tree
graphical expression of its scream as I incise myself transversely
growth rings
the effect of shortcut—accelerate hair
from growth movement
from movement the impression   of mental motivation
                                       of communication

by hand of wholesnake
                —condemned to being a visionary
                —made to read in prescient eyes
outside these moments
                —stung by a bee (entrusted by the snake)

and by the sting
                —linked with her
in the motion of membranous wings
                —cooled down
in melting between two shapes
                —stopped

in animal
         head bent
bat-blind
         eyes glow
through sharp shards of the landscape
run in the line of the scent

something huge
in human things that one cannot be rid of at once
flush out through sharp blades of grass
one can beat it under the threshold of insignificance

indestructible

( )

One side is tirelessness
the other: tiring
closing the door
in front of me and behind me
without a difference I face
the call: 'Fold!' (into oneself inside oneself)
precedes the apotheosis of the labyrinth
a change, escalating: 'A wandering which
begins to follow rules
ceases to be . . . '
after the call: 'Unfold!'
I find myself in a labyrinth
      —smoothness itself
after the self-destruction
      —something tender
like a gift of building oneself again
     re-es-table-ished
     behind the door
in the wardrobe
I wander through the folds of the hangings
ironing the labyrinth
returning to it the excessive human warmth
somewhere in the cooling process a way to
         embody

( )

The part of the landscape which I (with my body) obscure
is mortal
anchored by the roots of the nerves
you see me through absence
of the figure in the picture
through its silhouette
I traverse the line of fiction back and forth seamlessly
connecting with the horizon
my tendrils putting me in motion
I follow the light like an epileptic
searching for support: wrapping the ray
I lift myself to it: MEGARDEN IN THE AIR
uprooted   at the peak of the spasm
consciousness turns off
I get lost in myself: disreGARD IN GARDen

( )

So perfectly wrapped up not a bit in vain
and by that virtue replaceable
with the cobweb a hint of chorea-graphy
I'll weave into you or through you into another
warp and weft: attack of a scout bee
a kamikaze sent to die
on my doubting skin
magnetized needles treated by shade
and yet my knock on the casing
(asks about:) the one-way nature to the acoustics of the void
through the thready pulse unravelled in the opposite direction

('Or have other less
                hostile islands been palpated?')

(Universal Good Feeling)

it washes off equally intensely
soap
and
base stone

it narrows on my neck
a dangerous detail—provisionally the base
the chain persistently pressed
into finger pads

it carries my stairs atom by atom
on shoes in which nobody

by the furniture's tangents
pressed by its weight
they grew from the carpet—unripe from the unripe
I lost shades
red on red
like drops
on the single spine

Texturation: Something that occurred in the relationship between the table and the chairs. Gushed out of the dream, the floor, forced out by the weight of the furniture. (It) must have been growing in the shadows—of the table, of the chairs, enforced and enigmatic, caught in the act of living. In spite of the ties and owing to them, it divides into numerous new unfinished lives.

(Albino)

The holiday sank into a new spot
I'm being chased by a fissure
                             with a gift
the container is the contents
vital functions vacuum-sealed
anaesthetized from adversary effects
the gift itself—
                     begins with a look in time
unobtrusively like a leaf on a tree
the impression of the sun on the tissue
flashes—confirms, denies
my solubility:
                     at the bottom of the aquarium a lock
                     under the lid another surface

( )

I bite an apple
it withdraws
filled with primal fear
deflates
the bite hanging on a shred of skin
untransformed
before the mouthful, its blade gets invented
behind the blade a crater
a gesture frozen in lava
so fleeting
it can be considered a figment
so urgent
it can be made real

(Trompe-l'œil)

In place of the lamp a whale's heart
hanging on a thick vein
covered in phosphorescent spots
squirting measured doses of light
stains everything it hits
but it works oblivious to its mechanism
only the spots on the surface don't fit:
this is not a suit with a dead pattern
on a body too much alive
you can cut it and polish it like agate
but the spots remain
with the same emphasis
Perhaps they are not spots at all
Perhaps they are pores
so large in the moment of diastole
that they fit a whole hand
which the systole will lock in . . .

(Breathing Exercise)

From my side of the view
a tree behind the window
from the side of the tree
I slowly breathe out into apples
blowing them up from next to nothing
like too mild an illness
but like replacement lungs

I can't separate them from myself and know that it's not falling I need to do

but breathe in

everything

I breathed out before

( )

there is the density of locks
and the density of the gaps between the locks

notches don't lock into notches
there is no resistance
that's why I won't unlock the snow

a little yellow is enough
for that vast amount of white
it makes it possible to talk about otherness
it makes snow confit in its own juice
out of anger

pass through the hole between stones
painfully crawl through the gap
to be able to speak

pour oneself in and solidify in the space of the gap
by force of one's helplessness remain in it
transform stones into something else

( )

As I describe a non-existent drawing
the conditions of its birth enthral me
to draw an exterior around individuals
move at the command of individual objects
if I get in, I'll get in by force
through the opening I will screen my gaze with my eye
image..colourless juice
forehead..colour and where am I?
you sink into a soft sofa
it retreats with you in it
ahead of the retreat a heel
on my head a crowd of paranoiacs
a beast on six legs
pulling a fibre from you—wrapping itself
a cocoon
         without the meaning of a hidden life
         without surprise seeping through
'You ball!'

(A Weight)

Quite calm I let
objects and people disappear inside me
sweet and heavy volumes
distance inside me after each
clots its colourless blood

It's an echo of a movement
a force lurking from the picture:
whom I love I freeze

mirror's tense muscle
sympathetic to breaking point

My interest is cold
in the cone of my ice
don't breathe . . . and drops of mercury
slip out to longed-for orbits
like long-withheld warmth

(Performance with Lazarus)

'... he both exposes and protects
himself from our gaze
performing a mirror image of
the danger (we) pose:
through the prism of his own death
he inspects his body
with unusual cruelty'

. . .

I'm lying on the floor
parallel with the wall

Reduced to the elementary gesture

I lend myself
To similarity

. . .

Sitting by the window
I stitch a Stigma onto my body
(it is shaped like a fissure)

large
red   (this sort of pain)
theatrical

(that detaches you from its cause)

a number of short
unrelated
stabs

(from your)

( )

Between me and the object of research
is nothing.
The distance is included in me,
completely.
Between me and the object of research
there is no difference, no space.
The object of research is a suction cup
draining the distance.
It is my presence
which I decided
not to disrupt.

(today, another step)

this lace is a code for sitting
and I'm an acrobat
on the backrest of your chair
you turn and stand up and don't recognize
the day has passed
not a second clean in me
my stomach smiles at you
my ritually lacy
smile by smile
the clot
a scene
of a vast space
(betweenus leads through me)
it got stuck in my lace
the clot
it moves, looks, sees
looks and sees
the moment of revelation
the thing not to be missed
the moment and a bit
we'll sit and wait

( )

Including a tiny fault
was necessary
as was wrapping to the consequences
and creating Lazarus around it
disappearing in his act

repeat repeat
shout into the shelter

(This forest this garden)

This forest cannot be rained through
each in own bubble
we cannot hide

Here you can still see the garden rushing
a small
shred of a frozen lake in its mouth

it will not break a hair of the forest

it only glances back: 'Look, a garden!'
when the running weight smashes into a trunk

and spits out
the small shred of a frozen lake

once again
the running weight into the trunk

and swallows
what it bit

Facelessness
(2004)

All that compacts itself is bidding for its own heart At a hollow control centre Plucking up the courage for the first decisive strike—not too strong, since it impresses the one and only—in a striking but dead form—stamp Nor too weak, else it dissolves in the always flowing flux and whirl It must strike with measured emphasis Provide the first impulse Oscillate into a series of imprinting-flowing forms

—

(perhaps) I'll essay myself
but how and what self?
I hold no confidence in this matter
despite that
I'll try to plant confidence within me
uproot first—then plant
plant myself in words/plant among the words
speak myself out of the word/sprout through to the roots

similar to the word—
precise in a sense
and in nonsense—
wounded with precision/I limp away on my own roots
                        I'll stand on the roots of the word

bare and on word's root
I'll take a stand against my own attempts

: will not want

—

May I? May I come at rest here? And once I get used to inertia, I'll let myself go again

—

almost
in the tightest closeness of the tightest closeness
under the attentively smoothened surface
a tiny sudden folding
or rather a slight recess
it could be almost anything
lips, a mouth
a base of a deadly injury
an intensely felt confidence:
the unnameable fell onto me
and here, through here threads into me
and here and here
it has penetrated me thoroughly

—

fluent is the water
rising and turning glassy
glazing pores and
broken surfaces

you go through feelings: you do not wake

the automatic trigger
a fragment of a movement and nothing
that would precede it nothing
that it would precede
just shameless choreography
arms and legs
spread in a puppet's scream

sounds budding under the skin
oils of light burst
sealed in a cloudy flow

—

Diverting attention I describe myself as an injury A cut in the skin The feeling of pain, more monotonous than fateful, shines through the defining contours of the description, failing to comply with the data of a sharply outlined shape provided by vision And when from the broken skin a flood of inarticulate sounds surges—it is me trying to speak to you after a long time—a single closeness might heal it—and again it is you—with no shape to hide yourself Undescribed and indescribable A spectre of a winner The moment you move away, it is your voice in which I speak, your tongue I need to renounce myself, not give myself away, stick my tongue back in the mouth and cover it with my hand I need to silence myself to be able to speak

—

'For only where I lose my firm contours I start making sense,'

                                          I say

I say, but I don't align myself with myself

—

at the beginning I erect a wall the fissure
in which I disappeared

in the dream's consciousness I break the feigned sleep

Stepping out of the fissure
I peeled off chipped from the rule of the wall
born and exposed
in the comic of the moment

blurred out of focus, long and in motion to one place exposed

a ball shot through a fissure / invades the thin air / breaks the skin on the milk / and jumps around the room / posing danger to all fragile objects / in their sovereignly own / threatened places / itself so unseemly / discouraged by the wall

skin skinned in skintight skinned in skin skintight skinned in skin skinned in skintight skin skinned in skintight skinned in skin skintight skinned in skin skinned in skintight skin skinned in skintight skinned in skin skintight skinned in skin skinned in skintight I am here I am the voice pressed to the wall I am here I breathe through the pattern of your wallpaper I breathe in through the centres of the flat paper flowers I breathe deeply breathing in when you are not looking sunny afternoon roams my tongue my palate by roaming it thickens skin skinned in skintight skinned in skin skintight skinned in skin skinned in skintight by roaming it darkens I breathe out from the depths of my poisonous centres I cry milk in milk blood in blood but in tears I know no limits there are no limits and there is no limitation for the depth of this greedy feeling I am mourned and cannot stop it skin skinned in skintight skinned in skin skinned in skintight skinned in skin skinned in skintight skinned in skin where are you? skintight skinned in skin skinned in skintight skinned in skin skinned in skintight skinned in skin skinned in skintight skinned in skin skinned in skintight I am still here skin skinned in skintight skinned in skin skinned in skintight skinned in skin skinned in skintight skinned in skin skinned in skintight skinned in skin skinned in skintight skinned in skin skinned in skintight skinned in skin and what are you doing? skintight skinned in skin skinned in skintight skinned in skin skinned in skintight skinned in skin skinned in skintight skinned in skin skinned in skintight skinned in skin skinned in skintight skinned in skin skinned in skintight skinned in skin skinned in skintight I resemble skin skinned in skintight skinned in skin skinned in skintight skinned in skin skinned in skintight skinned in skin skinned in skintight skinned in skin skinned in skintight skinned in skin skinned in skintight skinned in skin skinned in skintight skinned in skin skinned in skintight skinned in skin skinned in skintight skinned in skin skinned in skintight skinned in skin skinned in skintight skinned in skin skinned in skintight skinned in skin skinned in skintight

what are you mixing?   I'm putting words together those that don't catch on
fall off   it speaks and it bites
                              it frightens it makes you laugh
                         it's a trick it's a wonder
I both get up and stay put   loop in loop
under the lid of the ancient soup   that which touches me and that which
does not
under the glass   a mouth
mechanically chattering its teeth   it speaks it bites
I float even as I walk on a pane of glass
just above the mouth in a lasting vertigo
                         it's a trick it's a wonder
                                        wander
                                            water
we've already cast our nets   —water
                         —air
                              —safety

—

a hit in the invisible
headlong scurrying body
in the white target
a hit that sets painful
boundaries, makes visible, tints with contrast,
pushes, prods on the scale of
visibility, it is a place, an opening
aperture, something after all, a source of
images, a crater of imagery which
only needed to be opened
a wound—   a mosaic
             inlaid with mirror
                'the mystery of the body' as she said later

—

squatting at the edge, I lift creatures from boiling water, the surface is soft, open; still reaching out, also in cold water, when the surface closed, skinned over thick with my image; besieged: like when on a snow-covered yard they slip off the glove from a scalded hand, facing, towards, through myself I tear

—

countless voices have spoken inside me at once

words divide me into pieces

(but my) hand does not move
does not record

—

my morning feels as if it was snowing through my spread fingers the whole night as if the snow kept vigil into me the whole night as if it was me who had whipped all this confectionary beauty from my weakening frog body's proteins as if the whole night I was hiding (from myself) a freezing object in a firm grip

. . . imprecisely I remember

—

face open in a protective gesture of covering:
face falling back to the cause

—

under the touch of the word I wish to escape, I freeze,
twice present

—

as I speak I change into I change into I change into

—

now, I do not wish to know (how and of what it was made), I just wish to go back there

—

there: where I have never been before
here: where I am now
and there and here: where I am all the time

—

What is necessarily above the surface then is not (my) face It is a mask of water floating on the surface A strange occurrence: a wrinkled surface, fashioned water The thing under the surface: water in water

Why should the face be an exception? Why should the face be an exception from the surface? Why couldn't the change of expression, at other times the sign of the inner life of its carrier, for now be just a sudden and chance wrinkling of the surface touched by the wind?

—

face down
drop by drop
poured into
the prepared surface

face up
headfirst
poured
sharply
breathed in

—

north, as the destination—a vision cursed and frozen in distance which cannot be covered

the point with which I wish to merge, which I wish to become, is unable to resist my attacking otherness for long and—penetrated by my unrest, it begins to divide—it splits and folds the compact northern sphere

the shocking motley of the shades of white, the thousand scents of the snow, crests of the drifts making sounds to the touch

—

come to me—stay away

—

I stretch arms into void
they hesitate
one of many faces rouses

I am
    not who
        I am
            not where

—

we can watch the movie
together and/or
in between

between us
is not complicated

from the
right side of the
projection screen

to kill with a shadow—
malevolent
and yet gentle

the clearest evidence
gone missing
from the case

a finger—like a needle pointing through the eye:
an imprint—
by a back
projection
of a movement
etched
from the retina
. . .
pit the fruit
close the lids

smoothly and movingly
melt
                (on the tongue)
to weave
double
presence
into one
muffled
                demise
with airy blue thread
      intimately and indistinctly
   (such is the meaning of this expression now)
it drips
into us
            the silent fickle death
and:
perhaps
it won't be
possible
to reversibly
unwind
into the wind

—

you say that gestures—too many gestures—divert attention from what needs to be said; you say: today again you look at me with suspicion; as we keep gestures to the minimum, the force pours over and concentrates into words, into that which we wish to say, only then our speech is firm and convincing, you say—you make no gestures, hands on the table, one palm up, I look into it as you talk, lines in it: drawn firmly, without a tremble, reduced to the bare minimum; I listen: you speak firmly and convincingly, you speak and I listen—with absent-minded gestures under your voice I palpate: grooves and curves, cat backs of conjunctives, weak spots of insecure and flattering bonds, I let it slide under my hands, I let it—hot and silken—roam into my ears

Parcelling Out the Air
(2007)

panther

each cell in my body
is a small black panther
and all at once they bang their paws
at millions of my doors
one scary panther
—huge effect
of mass turmoil—
putting its needle-claws
to the spinning disc
dropping a cutting hair
into the tense tissue

black panther
trapped by scissors
in a paper silhouette
isolated
in an infection ward

in a tight house of glass
under the cloak of breath
prowling like predators
the heavily starched buds
grow into skin

a shell

I throw the body
off a cliff
into sleep
seagulls take it to pieces
as it dives through the air
or keep it just above the water
secured with their beaks like pegs
cleansed of its own blood
Shroud of Turin
restlessly I squirm I sound
and dry into thin shivers
like a shell driven out of its mind
fitful unrest
prevents the face from healing
water works on it
and sleep
like a shivering surface
gives it back a hundred times
changed beyond recognition
and I push it away a hundred times
like a plate of food
I don't want
don't want to eat

shiver

at first, I didn't notice a thing
I moved my arms legs
walked to and fro talked
laughed sobbed
and used the instruction manual
instead of the missing script
and used the instructions for use
as instructions for use
only when I took off the gestures
like swollen jewels
and shifted the body to darkness
when it was its turn
I noticed
the weak but persistent shiver
and with a sharp clarity I watched
individual grains crumble
from eroded sections
I watched them slide and fall
into living tissue
I watched the body in panic get adorned
and fight the darkness in the dark
with a thin layer of nacre

livid

untouched
immersed
in (your) presence
like a pallid spot
in the petals'
soft glow

it rained
and I was unable to show
the slightest fragment
of the pale story

I just swiftly
laid the little
dead woman
on the top
shelf of the fridge
next to the yogurts eggs
and opened jars
of preserves

then the rain began
and I could not
develop it further

in the petals' soft glow:
as if I was ashamed
of the fact that now
it is still not alive

parcelling out the air

the curve of the bridge
biting the spotted neck
of the electrified night
while I wait
numb hands turn into disgusting buds
alveoli of sullen orchids
full
of sharp February air
air filled with cellophane
air filled
with projection screens
while I wait
they all unfold
thinly cut
like slices of cold
buffet meat

tulips

the metal click
of the diaphragm lamella
of the central shutter lamella
three and three (segments of the perianth)
set
according to measured
parameters of light
darkness in the mouth
and around it an instant aureole
you tell me: think of me
I think: I tend to you
like water tends to its favourite stone:
it caresses and keeps wearing down
until there remains
no special feature
no edge
clear sound
nothing like you
inwards in each
of the swinging heads
a small exposed face
not willing to pass into nothing:
think of me think of me

bulbs

in the tightest urgent closeness
I eagerly gather light residues
stuck in skin grooves and folds
and down in the heavy darkness settled at the bottom
I store precious sugars in polished bulbs
and then waste everything lavishly in a single stroke
at the alarmed flicker of the beacons
and warning blare of sirens
when a flood of lurid tulips
rushes from the cut skin into the silence
whole flocks of these perfidious creatures
which in childhood I, bravely facing
the enormous patch,
with one flick of the wand
en masse unmasked

roundness

all those rotting fallen and the ones we bit and threw away
instantly skinned over—the fruit skin tightened and brightened
they flew up and now they float around us like bubbles
air made of real water and nutritious plankton
we keep going straight unnoticed we return
to the starting point crash into new clusters
of gliding fruit clashes are muffled but perceptible
smells get released mixed and dispersed
from these moments if we gathered them
if we threaded them on a single floating fibre
they might last to eternity

sweet and dear

at the fatal crash, fiercely revived beauty
a deer in the passenger seat
hoofs of frost on the windscreen
of the angular white Mercedes
a box of frost flowers
on the way to the unknown recipient
I seem unable to tune the car radio, all this static
the antlers wrapped in frost it's beginning to snow
snowflakes in the wind like arrows mark
the direction of the ride so eagerly
that from the inside it looks
as if suddenly we
came to a complete halt

happyend

a roused fleeing of fish
from a nose-dive
projecting it in slow motion
I take scissors and my cold hand
cuts my screens
in thin silver strips
which flutter in the wind
which glitter in the light
which scare off the birds

beckett's horses

I sit on a bench
light up blow out
and flick
instantly pigeons
sneak up and flock around
stepping carefully
as if their feet were covered
in sensitive baby skin
those most ordinary grey
always sickly-looking
town pigeons watch me
look at me like horses
at beckett—unsettlingly
irritated each separately
and all at once like well-
assembled parts
of a detection device

public park

words rolling like drops of water on greased feathers
I get lost in the merging skin of a foreigner. an excess
from which at noon I erect a glimmering tent
driving filthy weeds out to the misty bank of language
today misses me, the chance passer-by
on the periphery of yesterday. I slouch to the public park
where I don't: get in touch, take roots
develop things, let anyone feed me
thank, say hello, where I just silently easily
breathe, so you can't tell with certainty
which of the many species I actually belong to

coastal research

a hero lost between two events, two scenes
as if time didn't matter; only the spaces: too hot or cold
waiting rooms, spacious halls, emptied chambers, platforms out of use
but most importantly stuffy rooms without views, there he rests, there
    he remains
the unhero in his unstory, there he holds his opinion as if time (never)
    mattered at all
nor one of its impenetrable dimensions; only the adjustable armchairs
the sofas covered in supple leather, not the galloping days, only the
    tame sofas
on short unshod legs. growing into the floor
or sneakily shuffling around
feel free to approach them, touch them, dare them
all without the usual spurs and the extremely critical vigilance

calligraphy

in a heartbeat the distant
swaps with the close
a multiplied echo
does not fade but stays
a concentrated coarsened
armoured
rose of the depths, or onion
and someone from a distance
writes to you in clear ink
on the skin marks of another's
sorrow

dragonflies

as contours lose definition the blue
soaks in the grey the wind's palm caresses
bristled straw needles light recasts them
into a silvery lake we waver above
the impassable surface and flail
like precious spoons we dig deeper
and pass

Coastal Research
(2009)

~

on the way to the destination I generate fatigue
fatigue is then a truer destination
than the city to which I am headed

anytime anywhere
I'm able to lose orientation

~

in the hotel room
I stand by the window for a while
trees move behind the double glazing
the wind in the leaves is mute
neither whisper
nor sighs
remind me of this absence
the fatigue that has now
disengaged from me
is more real
than what lies
ahead of me

~

fatigue duplicates
events repeat

events
as if always already repeated

as if there were
no first times

again
as if

the difference is subtle but noticeable
glass pane another glass pane

and between them a distance
a gap inserted between the past

and present event
dielectric

fatigue is more real
reality more fragile

glazing is double
difference subtle

~

in the middle of the city
in the middle of the day
I reach my hand

a glass pane
another glass pane

I don't notice the difference
and estimate distance inaccurately

at noon
at the margins
of the street
trees move

it still rains

quickly we run
to the taxi waiting outside

from behind
over his shoulder
I watch the road

always ahead
towards a conclusion

behind the glass trees move

in the rear mirror
a fragment of reality

between us
something shapeless

it still rains

at the arranged time
I stand at the arranged place

shake hands
say my name

a fragment of reality
projected onto a different time

~

reaching out I wish
for the same thing to happen again
in reality as in a mirror
I don't add only remove
drink from a cup unwrap leaf through
put away layers of the yellowed white
deposits of dusty air
and cyanotic buzzing
wiping traces of breath from in front of my mouth
I step back from the doubled glass panes
flies wither between them
certain colours repeat again and again behind them
outside trees move they shed leaves
touch so unlike touch
you almost can't feel it
equally I want
and don't want
I want and don't want to be
in the cramped hotel room
and on the beach by the sea
equally alive and dead

~

the thing in between

in between
even without our
efforts

does not remain the same
it changes

on the beach by the sea
and in the cramped hotel room

between the ceiling of indeterminate colour
and beige velour carpet

between flow and ebb

we expend
much energy
to prevent it

anxiously
repeating the same actions
applying the same formulas

the result nonetheless is never
quite the same

~

surfaces shapes bodies
brisk and drowsy
semiautomatic

microorganisms
establish secret colonies

the dragging beginnings of future disasters
irreversible dulling—weariness

things losing their contours
under a sticky film

faces behind the glass

under thin ice
shallow water breathes

to touch to smell to taste

fill air with germination
and funny yelling

I haven't decided yet
again: I hesitate & mislead
but: repeat actions gestures

gingerly inspect a distant object
it resembles a sea shore

glitter the waves of new foliage
flicker the motor vehicles

quiet cloudless dogs vanish behind the corner

dreams of rooms

in between is a distance
hard and fragile

glass wall
on which breath condenses (does not mix)

hot—cold
hazy images of parallel worlds
passions liquefied at the bottom

(in which dream did I before leaving
water the plants close the windows
but forget to turn off the light
switch off the radio?)

time that needs to be filled
and can no longer be counted on

to connect with a finger
drops attached to the surface

let trickle
pass

~

yes of course
if it's fine tomorrow

but
tomorrow will not be fine

or perhaps
it will be fine after all

and even if
it isn't fine tomorrow

surely
it will be some other time

but
what follows from that?

how to connect this with that
and reach a conclusion?

~

between me
and different me

between the ceiling of indeterminate colour
and beige velour carpet

in one of the countless identical rooms
on the rock the size of the tennis court
on the shore of endless worlds

from fragments images fantasies
I compose

experiences and events
which never happened

coastline

sounds as I wake up
while I still can't
distinguish
one from the other

I can't be certain
about
the originator
source
distance
of the sound event

in the morning
still darkness
I wake up to
someone sobbing near me
it might even be me

it takes me a while
to calm down

to make sure
that not me
not near me

not sobbing
but the radio playing

~

learning by heart
the mark
on the ceiling
above the bed

you can see it
even if it wasn't there

like a flower
in a vase
on the table

it opens

spreads fragrance
anxiety

learn by heart
and not abandon

life
bounded
by the margin of a stain

Works & Intimacy
(2012)

***

the carpet wears out
PVC flooring shrinks
glass doesn't mist
pot plants water themselves
bedsheets don't follow fashion trends
women's hats suffer a lot
men's hats often sweat through
shoes squeak
hanging loops on coats tear
wool products need soft water and soap
starched linen holds its shape
it's the 'little things' that matter
hair ages
the body changes as years go by
perfume accompanies the woman
potatoes go black
chives help digestion
mayonnaise thickens
cream-based sauces burn
juice doesn't leak
milk gets sour
mature cheese has a pungent odour
soft dough sticks to the pastry board
braided bread rises
rice is seeming
pasta increases its volume
gooseberries keep
fruit turns into jelly
plums replace apricots
fats 'smoke'

vegetables change colour
vitamin C is destroyed
a small glass of wine conjures up a pleasant aroma
fish is indispensable
appetiser refreshes
dessert reveals
fruit plays a clear role
coffee is preparing
bananas are sensitive to low temperatures
greens dry the carrot root
game becomes tastier
a light raincoat doesn't weigh us down
work uniforms meet the standards
decorations make cleaning difficult
budget helps
marriage starts
marriage ends

***

once the stain dries, it's difficult to clean
a brushing door can damage the carpet
mosquitoes are very nasty insects
the bathtub is smooth, you can slip easily
after drying out, the fingerprint effectively disappears
portable light fittings are very practical
washing lace is very delicate
accessories are an important part of every outfit
frowning is incompatible with anything we spoke about

***

allergic rash
fever diseases
pots with limescale
carpet stained with wine, beer, fruit juice, etc.
nosebleed
dizziness of the milder type
occasional insomnia
saggy curtains
parquets with greasy stains
chapped lips
dust in the eye
glass dirty with fly droppings
wood decay in walls
faded paintings
rusty iron objects
stomach and intestinal cramping

***

choose very wisely
carefully trace
blend it gently
mustn't be visible where
the makeup begins
and where it ends

***

banana stains on children's clothes
with boiling milk
in a hot solution
fresh stains
blueberry
urine
we can also
with salt which absorbs
cotton wool wrapped around a piece of wood
after using petroleum cleaner
with washing up liquid foam
spoon with a cloth
lipstick stains
in lukewarm water
on delicate fabrics
stains like maps
if the character of the fabric permits it
repeat the process

***

crystal will be clear and sparkling again
the silver will no longer be tarnished
chewing gum will peel off on its own

sweat-stained and faded parts
however, can never be removed

Tianni is truly a natural beauty with a kind, sweet and caring spirit

```
          s smooth       st          pigm        scarr
       help        pro           con        min      right
       kin     ill     to e      th gorg    g    on    er    .
I   art     shape    fill   e e e row  w    pik   pen
full           define  look        ow        nish   ff   neat-
         edge        ARS cream  conceale         me    m   e
              tra   p             trick       o   re in need
       id              me   do      tart      rim      e eye
       he used           late    shadow         ocket    tran-
s       lo    I      uffed                      colour
concentrate        inner            er of the    This
and    iss        at is us      ar   t   oft      ook  To b
       e intens   in the inner and outer
             Lady         plum      ad    real         look  I
wanted                      lips         I
mat e          want      make              's
         smooth                      's       & P      ip
     foll         ARS    m ed   l et   att    p P
line    ps              uff      out       , I          C
Recoll           e c   t      lip     soft         edges.
```

Celeste is the mum, so we're gonna make her glamorous

```
First       n  d         d a lit       moi  ur  er      hat
like              give         glow                     thing
         beauty                   found     , and it looks
     light       a   ble  d              match
just  utt   just   itt    it           at           lids  ext
       just        top right       line           line  So this
is    h                  er        really              so
            you're doing other people's
y                onom                y        well   fit
hand             hard                         id
see                         she doesn't              id
                      thick line                     drag
      eye  down                    coat   masc
Mary             Masc              fill          rows
           un    shadow         angled            fill
nice full arch                  set everything with bronzer
            her lips              taupe    er    ink
  rks   ally nice   kind          mension       lip
                 bit        now                    bit
    light                    lip          setting everything
with setting spray
```

Coralie has vivacious personality and a very big and kind heart

```
A         needed more mo    re        add           her
A         is a novice                 many              s on
    s    prim     eye       ban      Eye P     P      all
over              us     mb     gh    esh    w       lid
softly  end          socket            blend       tiq
   he         I th    in    he yes         lack Long Last
   l Lin   this is great for    one                 it  runny
eye         finish the eye        sed   shing    l e  ash
  ar       e                              ash          sure
that the                                Orange
                       very dark and also
It is important t       t  t         th      d th    e    e
                    e    e    e     e   e    excess
            make sure        seemless I concealed
              This            under        and     an  d
           light  on her face          bright coral
           she loved      very l       I    e    give
               lease of life and a deeper           o Lip
           o line the lips               o    o
           oral  o give it a little more     o        o
on top
```

A Public Dictionary of Intimacy

(fragment)

And let no one tell me anymore that it wasn't a great love, because each love is the greatest.
Are you also one of those couples that, besides spending nice moments together, set another goal—to conceive a child?
If your husband starts turning into another man, it could be more than a midlife crisis.
How is it that such age-disparate couples don't end up on the ash heap of relationships after a few crazy weeks?
But then she met Karol online and started a hot adventure with him...
But I must admit, the disgust I felt during physical intimacy was indescribable.
Only when she got rid of a huge pile of fat did she realize that unforeseen possibilities were opening up before her.
He takes medication, doesn't cause problems, but nobody knows about his life outside the surgery.
I can't go out without pantyhose, my legs are covered in spider veins.
I'm worried I'll never be happy.
He was like a lamp attracting nocturnal moths.
She was beautiful and incredibly sexy, so I went after her.
Bangs, noise, jumping, ball throwing, pulling and rearranging tables, chairs, etc. above our heads at three in the morning, in the afternoon, in the evening, and sometimes even at night make our living very unpleasant.
I couldn't see through tears at all, I have no idea how I got home.
Can my problem be fixed surgically?
We got talking and every day we got closer.
I penetrated my previous partner fully in the classic position, but not the current one, she says it hurts her.

We hadn't even finished our coffee when he started harassing me.

The music played. We cuddled together as if we had known each other since birth. My icy heart began to melt. I knew I would fulfil all of this man's desires.

Is it normal that I don't want to go on a date with someone I don't like?

Every day we work on our relationship, and it's the best job I've ever had.

Losing all your hair over the course of a year is very difficult to cope with. I don't want to end up bald.

How many nights my daughter and I cried! If her tears and mine were combined, it would already be quite a stream.

Who would have thought that she would eventually turn into a sex-hungry slut?

Lenka loves domestic animals, but she's troubled that she can't properly clean the sofa even with the vacuum cleaner.

But a man isn't a gas stove that you can simply turn off. When his instinct kicks in, it's as if he loses control over himself and can't be stopped.

But these are more nails in the coffin of their cohabitation and love.

I had unprotected sex with a random partner.

I had four beautiful children and a loving husband . . . I lacked nothing for happiness . . .

I had a strange premonition that something would happen, I attributed it to my female intuition.

I have vices like any other person, so occasionally I indulge in a cod in mayonnaise.

I like it when there's action in love.

Should I apply special cosmetics?

His wife gave him twins.

I often reward my wife. They don't have to be expensive gifts, frequently a sincere look is enough.

My husband is a good person.

My world collapsed in one second. I sat there desperate, humiliated, destroyed.

We must protect her and stand by her. We'll do everything to help her.

We thought that with our love and care we would help him, he would feel good and grow into a good person. How will we cope with him?

Do you think it's okay for him to still be interested in sex at his age?

I wear thick socks to bed at night and I'm still cold.

His children sang and cried at his funeral in a live broadcast.

I behave in the sun as my skin allows.

At first, I was curious if it even works. Then I convinced myself that it works. Now I wonder what the final result will be. I've started the second package now, my breasts have already increased by one size and are still slightly growing.

I caught my husband in bed with my friend.

However, our marriage was already crumbling shortly after the wedding.

When I was with her I had nothing to talk about. But she did. I mean, she talked about what she saw or did in the morning and what she did in the afternoon.

It doesn't happen to me when I look at other girls. Only with her. When I hug her, when I see that she's nicely dressed, I immediately get an erection.

He constantly complains about something, I have to fetch his pills, it's almost impossible to get him to practice hygiene and I can't stand it.

However, the bride soon showed her true colours, and unfortunately, not even beautiful grandchildren could stop the family disaster.

Sometimes I don't expect his touch, and when he touches me, I recoil in fear.

I never thought I would fall in love after fifty.

We enjoyed the period of sweet secrecy with my partner very much.

She accepted a new challenge in life. And that challenge was to seduce me . . .

She refuses to sit in front of the mirror and dye her roots every three weeks.

He begged, brought flowers and as he said himself, he wished to save the family.

We hit it off, and since then, we've been living for each other.

There's an unpleasant smell spreading from the sink drain in Mrs Mária's kitchen and she can't get rid of it.

I accentuated my lips and cheeks in a juicy raspberry shade.

After a long time, I was with someone who was a friend, a lover, and a husband all in one person.

After much deliberation and many tears, we decided that we don't want to interfere with nature.

I ruined my life.

Why are men afraid of me?

I blush in the presence of a naked woman.

But four days have passed, and he hasn't called. What went wrong?

Dressed as a woman, he snuck into the bathroom and listened to them urinate.

At the simplest movements, at the most innocent words, I trembled all over.

My boyfriend is amazing, he tries very hard, but to me, it feels more like a sport than enjoyable lovemaking.

It came somewhat naturally.

Although my breasts are smaller, I like them. I wouldn't want them to be different.

I enjoy sports, and sometimes I feel like I sweat too much.

He slipped and fell in the bathtub in the morning.

I split the bread roll in half to feel like there are two.

I've been married for three years to Alenka. A nice girl, the best I've ever met.

With Marta, we're connected by some invisible thread that can't be broken by distance, passing years, wealth, or illness.

I'm unhappy with my feet.

I stood there dazed, but then the tightness in my chest suddenly eased, and I let out a hysterical scream.

He was a shadow of his former self.

That's what life wanted.

Pregnancy is my private matter, which, I hope, won't reflect in my work.

Now I have a new acquaintance. It almost came to lovemaking, but I backed off. I wanted to, but I couldn't.

I rejoiced in every little thing, and he rejoiced in my bright eyes . . .

For me, the fact that he wanted to cheat on me is the same as if he already did.

Choosing the right life partner is essential. Otherwise, I couldn't hold this position today.

He looks content and continues to live his immoral life.

I'm certainly not the type of woman who strictly adheres to one pattern.

In a moment of weakness, we decided to go on a joint vacation as a couple, which is already paid for, but now I'm scared.

They lived a nice, content life, and now should be suing over an old house and an old car?

I could endure a lot, from her and from life.

I know I'm difficult, but perhaps he'll manage . . .

He says he doesn't want to hurt the children. But he also doesn't want to see a specialist.

Everything was ideal; I felt a miraculous lightness of being and a thrill from every glance or touch of his.

It's been about a month since it happened, but at that time it felt like he put a knife in my heart.

I clear my mind with an evening walk, meditation under the stars . . .

Will her long-distance relationship last?

From a cup of coffee, it turned into a few glasses of wine over time, from glasses into day trips and dinners, and now we're slowly planning our wedding.

In those two years that we haven't seen each other he matured a lot and he especially became more manly in character.

We talked, later met at a disco, sparks flew, and that was it.

She held her breath and deceived her body.

She seasoned the sauce poorly, dressed inappropriately, didn't teach the children the poem he selected, didn't wipe the table.

I marvelled at his knowledge of stars or animals.

Contemporaneities
(2021)

this is about revival, a new renaissance
our present is
an influx of fresh blood

on an evolutionary higher level
foundations have been laid for new cultural advances
a new attitude towards life has become clearly unavoidable
the form it takes is the new superstructure and the new man

our schools keep producing fresh supplies of new cadres
under new slogans
they fight for new art

the new advanced taste
rings with fresh optimism

today when the new art is being made
today more than ever before

Szabó is stuck in yesterday

1953

the present looks into the past
and asks
how we managed to meet the goals
set for our organization by the resolution on development

there are new buildings and constructions
new premises for supply
new premises for maintenance and repairs

the new production and assembly plant
was stocked with new basic equipment

new construction increased capacity
for the treatment and recreation of our workers

the function of water manager has also been added

let us keep in mind these
dynamics of development
7.74 million CSK
745 thousand tons
38 grain silos

however, the finishing process is not over
the current base must continue to be not only expanded
but above all modernized

what specific tasks
are waiting for us in the near and distant future?

complexes that are significantly behind schedule
must be put into operation

in Železovce, Galanta, Trnava, and Hadovce
it is necessary to fix what can still be done

despite a significant step forward
our capacities are not sufficient

there is no effective way yet
of extending time

so let us focus instead
on the development of the mechanical loader
with electric drive

behind everything that has been done in the past
that we are currently doing
and will do in the future
we must always see man and people

1988

even today, there are regions in Slovakia
where the people live in very inadequate conditions
in great backwardness
a book was written once, What Hinders Slovaks
it held a mirror to the Slovaks
because we lacked the courage
to admit our faults
today there are other reasons
which hinder the development of the nation
our work today is primarily hindered
by ourselves again
one hinders the other
and then he cannot work for the nation
today we find ourselves in a position
which we have never been in before
today we have a wealth of resources
such as we never had before
but it cannot be said
that we are using them well
although it was not possible for us
to correct all our flaws
in such a short time
but it must be said
that we could have already done more

1922

the avalanche once in motion is hard to stop
a revolutionary shock wave knocks down the glass castles of aesthetic rules
restless process of accelerated autopoiesis

it's hard to transform a closed circle to a straight line
at the Smolenice conference on the role of artistic avant-gardes we attempted

work that provides a springboard for the artistic present
discloses new programmatic stimuli
regular international festivals and exhibitions
strengthen our hold on positions most recently won
fervently delving into new artistic tendencies

naturally, the pioneers are not to blame
nor are the generations of their artistic fathers and grandfathers
living their last days now

we are dealing with new elements
of the latest artistic development
with possibilities of new combinations
of fresh and intense impulses

new and still newer means and materials are sought
the technical inventiveness of the artist today knows virtually no bounds
textiles, plastics and metals, chemicals
water, fire, and other untrammelled forces of nature
everything is involved in the creation of new reality

new beginnings ferment
reward us with a lasting experience

talking about the engagement of art on contemporary developments currently dynamically reshaping the whole society there are things to follow up all the honest and consistent efforts of the last decades when works were created that survived their time not by timelessness and neutrality but by passionate participation in the struggle of workers for a better future it has already been stated that art also went through its crisis in our country for the artist an artistic crisis is usually also a personal crisis this must be understood because the artistic process is not lying in a bed of roses we the citizens of this country are not indifferent to the fate and mission of the artist if we want to help him humanely it does not mean just kiss away his wounds we stand for such a creative process the fruit of which will be new art today we are fighting for with those convinced and active artists today we are concerned with supporting their civic involvement with the full breadth of their talent we make no secret of the fact that we really want to captivate and excite artists for the great ideas of our time hundreds of millions of the most conscious self-sacrificing most progressive people on our planet are working and fighting for these values today the advantages of practical socialism are becoming increasingly visible to the whole world workplaces apartments housing estates schools roads everything must be constantly cultured it is necessary because it will increasingly appear as an internal need of working people

we are going through difficult times
worries press in on us from all sides
but a woman remains a woman
whatever happens in the world around her
she will always pay extra attention to fashion
and try to keep up with it
the fashion industry continues its work
as if nothing had happened
and produces ready-made miracles
now in Paris they are hard at work preparing
marvels of spring fashion

1944

today even politicians understand
the connection between economy and culture
creativity in today's society
becomes the engine of innovation
today we can count
a whole range of economic indicators
from the price of the work itself
or the ticket
up to the known multiplier effects
which cultural managers
know by
heart

the economy depends to a great extent on the level of reproductive performance which consists of the rapid recovery of sexual functions and timely and successful insemination the reproductive performance is low due to the long gestation period and relatively short life span and the efficiency of genetic progress is hindered by long generation intervals in the process of increasing intensification and rationalization controlled reproduction is a priority interference with reproductive functions leads to the maximum use of natural reproductive potential and optimal productiiiiiiiiiiiiiiiiiiiiiiiiiiiiiiiiiiiiiiiiiiiiiiiiiiiiiiiiiiiiiiiiiiiiiiiiiiion

let's harness the zeal of the young
let's use their energy which can be shaped in any way we want
where did this unusual feeling come from?
it is the vision of distant perspectives
it is the wireless telegraphy
everywhere there is an urgent need to change the soil
new soil from which our life will blossom to greater beauty
a state that we have not yet experienced
pure poetry
drowned in the brown and grey of the contemporary day
every Friday night
in the Metropol café
threads of impulses flutter through the ether
in poor studios
are already born
with new vigorous activity
the fruits of life's necessity
we will give up everything and toil
yes, we need a recast
in the fiery furnace of today's reality
today we won't be satisfied with surrogate
or a prescribed diet
we are healthy and hungry
we will not reproduce and copy
but create a new reality

1939

modern technology really demands
new forms of work organization
the basic assumption
is a carefully worked out plan
so that every worker knows his tasks
for the day, the week or a longer time
it is necessary to organie the work so
that the production plan is fulfilled evenly
every decade, day, shift, and hour

with the flame of the burner, comrade Vlach,
while demonstrating his method, levelled
a plate with dimensions 1,600 mm x 200 mm x 40 mm
in less than two hours
while straightening on the press
normally took eight hours

1957

as university employees
we were allowed to enter the building
where at the end of an empty corridor
we filled our time with planning

the ones who come after you will laugh at you the way you laugh at us now

option I: are we ahead of our times?
option II: are the times ahead of us?
    option III: . . . ?

the time is ripe for change
the system eroded by internal struggles has decayed
new culture opens wide horizons into the future
brings eternal dreams of freedom, happiness, and permanent peace closer
in the new society the mission of art broadens
the worker has become the centre of attention
art strives to make his life more beautiful
and teach him to see the familiar reality in a new way
in this way art participates in the creation of new reality
it does not just reflect it, but also remodels it
if the new art is to be worthy of its name
its form has to resonate with its new contents
the creation of the new style and new art
will become a creative process
marked by new artistic discoveries
this process will not dismiss
all that has been created before
but will build on
the art of the past and become
its organic continuation

today we must clean the temple of art of insects
and to the working and creative collectives return
what belongs unto it!

there is no time for whimpers, battles are tough and hard
what matters is the requirement of today
for today is the mater of the future
go out into the streets and plazas, to the factories and mines
sink your teeth into life's élan
and let yourself be impregnated by the social struggle of today
let its revolutionary spark burgeon in your blood!

this part of the world, exploited, proletarianized
and pauperized to the utmost measure
awaits its apostle—
the artist who would listen to the heavy heartbeat and breathing
of the worker and farmer collectives

our standpoint is crystallized and clear
today's despair must be strangled by the deed!

1925